Proofreading Theses and Dissertations

Second edition

Stephen Cashmore

Published in the UK in 2023 by
Chartered Institute of Editing and Proofreading
Studio 206, Milton Keynes Business Centre
Foxhunter Drive, Linford Wood
Milton Keynes
Buckinghamshire
MK14 6GD

ciep.uk

Copyright © 2023 Chartered Institute of Editing and Proofreading

ISBN 978 1 838358 26 6 (print)
ISBN 978 1 838358 27 3 (PDF ebook)
ISBN 978 1 838358 28 0 (ePub)

Second edition published 2023

First edition 2018: ISBN 978 0 993129 33 9 (print),
ISBN 978 0 993129 37 7 (ebook)

All rights reserved. No part of this publication may be reproduced or used in any manner without written permission from the publisher, except for quoting brief passages in a review.

The moral rights of the author have been asserted.

The information in this work is accurate and current at the time of publication to the best of the author's and publisher's knowledge, but it has been written as a short summary or introduction only. Readers are advised to take further steps to ensure the correctness, sufficiency or completeness of this information for their own purposes.

Typeset in-house
Original design by Ave Design (**avedesignstudio.com**)
Image credit: Creative Commons from Unsplash

Contents

1 | Introduction — 1

The purpose of this guide — 1
Definitions — 2
Proofreading or editing? — 2
Opportunities and risks — 4
Opportunities — 4
Risks — 5
Weighing it up — 6
How to get the work — 6

2 | Working with students — 8

Initial queries — 8
Warning flags — 10
Your response — 10
Calculating fees — 11
Student agreement — 13
Code of practice — 13
Academic agreement form — 13
Timing — 14
Workflow — 15
Version control — 16
Working on the sample — 16

3 | Ethical considerations — 18

Plagiarism — 19
Fact-checking — 21

Fact-querying	22
Common knowledge	22
Context and impact	23
Typographical error	25
Fact-querying summary	25
Artificial intelligence (AI)	26
How is AI going to affect proofreading theses and dissertations?	26
Using AI as proofreader	27
Using AI as copyeditor	28
Rewriting	29
References	30
Formatting	30
Code of practice	31
Academic agreement	34

4 | Summary   36

5 | The next step   37

1 | Introduction

The purpose of this guide

Why produce a guide specifically for proofreading or editing theses and dissertations? There are two reasons.

It is likely that your client – the student who has written the thesis or dissertation – will not have worked with a professional editor before. They will not know what information you need, how you work out your fee, what work you can do and what you cannot do, and your way of working. You will need to build a relationship with the student and at the same time introduce them to the world of professional editing. This is different from the situation when you are working with a professional author or publisher.

The thesis or dissertation has to be the student's own work. This means that you cannot alter the content, unless you judge it is a simple typographical error that needs correcting. And unless you have specific permission from the student's supervisor, you cannot substantially alter the wording. Again, this is significantly different from the situation where you are working on material for a book or journal article.

Both of these factors are discussed in this guide, but first some preliminary questions will be addressed:

- What are theses and dissertations?
- Do we proofread or edit a thesis or dissertation?
- What are the advantages and disadvantages of working on theses and dissertations?
- How do we get to work on a thesis or a dissertation?

Definitions

According to OED online, and conflating a couple of definitions, a 'thesis' is defined as:

> *A dissertation to maintain and prove a thesis (in the sense of a proposition laid down or stated, esp. as a theme to be discussed and proved, or to be maintained against attack); esp. one written or delivered by a candidate for a University degree.*

whereas 'dissertation' is defined as:

> *An extended scholarly essay, usually based upon original research, submitted for a degree or other academic qualification.*

These definitions don't make any specific distinction between a thesis and a dissertation. In fact, a thesis is described as a dissertation.

Nevertheless, in the UK a 'thesis' has come to mean a piece of original work written up for a PhD, and 'dissertation' has come to mean the same thing, only for work written up for Masters and other degrees below PhD level. Confusingly, in the US it is the other way around.

Throughout this guide 'thesis' is used to mean either a thesis or dissertation.

Proofreading or editing?

In a perfect world, a thesis will be presented to you in reasonable English, needing only a proofread – that is, correcting only for errors in spelling, grammar and punctuation, and pointing out inconsistencies and the odd awkward phrase or sentence. However, theses frequently need a lot more work than that.

This would not be a problem if this were, say, a technical book sent to you by a publisher for copyediting. It would be hard work, but you would

wrestle with the poor phrasing, incorrect word usage and faulty sentence structures, and attempt to make everything clear. But you should not normally do this for a thesis, because the work has to be the student's own: the more you change it, the more it becomes *your* work. There will be more about this complication throughout this guide, especially in '**3 | Ethical considerations**'.

For a thesis, what you may actually be doing is *proof-editing*; this term is defined in the CIEP course Proofreading 1: Introduction as:

> *the hybrid copyediting/proofreading tasks that many non-publishing organisations and private individuals require when they ask for proofreading services.*

Proof-editing entails addressing the usual proofreading concerns, but the level of intervention required may be much greater. How much greater can be difficult to pin down, and is discussed later in this guide.

For simplicity, the term 'proofreading' is used throughout this guide, though the actual work carried out may be simple proofreading, proof-editing or full-on copyediting.

Opportunities and risks

Opportunities

If you are busy, you can turn down a thesis without worrying too much about it, as a student, unlike, say, a publisher or journal author, is likely to be a one-off client.

However, if you do have time to give to a student, there is the possibility that they will come back to you when they write their first journal paper or book. They remember you. Proofreading theses and dissertations could be regarded as a form of marketing.

Similarly, some of your student clients might recommend you to friends and colleagues. Most students are part of large communities of fellow students and other academics, and a good deal of proofreading work on theses comes from word-of-mouth recommendations.

You can punch above your weight when proofreading theses: there is not the same pressure to understand the content that there is when working for a publisher or author. It goes without saying that unless you are a

polymath, you won't understand much of some of the theses you work on: they are, after all, meant to be cutting-edge research. But if you are working within the ethical constraints as described later in this guide, you should not be concerning yourself with content; you are proofreading for sense rather than accuracy. The same is not necessarily true for work coming from a publisher or author.

Proofreading theses will certainly put all your skills to the test. If you take on a handful of theses, you will quickly have to learn a great deal:

- how to respond to query emails that can be confusing, abrupt and usually short on information
- how to negotiate timing and fees
- how to strike up a working relationship with your student client
- how to make sure that you are working to a clear and ethical brief
- how to manage client expectations
- how to work in different formats
- how to decide what queries you can ethically make (and how to make them).

Risks

Generally speaking, your fee for carrying out the work won't be as good as you would get if you were working for a publisher or journal author. Negotiating a fee can also be tricky, because students generally do not understand what they are paying for (and perhaps more importantly, what they are not paying for because it is outside your remit), and because the thesis may not yet be completed, making it hard to work out an estimate.

The student you're working with might be poor at managing their time, and become increasingly anxious as their deadline approaches. If this happens you might find yourself working against the clock so that they can meet their submission dates.

As with other types of independent client, it is possible that a student will disappear without paying after you have carried out the work. This is rare,

and ways to reduce the chance of it happening are discussed later in this guide.

Some theses and dissertations are written in such poor English that it can be soul-destroying to edit them.

Some students might ask you to help them with formatting, which can be time-consuming and very frustrating.

Students might get upset when you stick to your brief and don't offer to 'help' them in any way that might be construed as unethical. They may then become frosty and the working relationship suffers.

Weighing it up

Overall, the advantages of working on theses usually outweigh the disadvantages. It's a steep but very fruitful learning curve for any editor. If you proofread diverse theses, your knowledge and confidence will grow. You may then feel more confident about working in new subject areas, or on multi-author works.

How to get the work

There is no easy formula to follow that guarantees you a thesis to proofread for a decent rate. Like any other search for any sort of editing work, first follow some basic tips:

1 | Introduction

- Make sure all your contacts know what you are looking for. Friends and relations – or the offspring of friends and relations – might be taking a degree; current or previous work contacts can also be a fertile place for enquiry.
- Make sure your website clearly flags up that you are happy to work on theses. For that matter, make sure that you have a website! Emphasise your academic experience. If you've got a degree or postgrad qualification, then put that on the About page, and mention experience of academic editing.

There are four other ways in which you might consider looking specifically for thesis work:

- Make contact with someone on the departmental staff at a university, and just ask. In these digital days, it doesn't even have to be a local university. It can be hard work trying to find the right person to talk to, but it can pay dividends. In particular, clarify the policy that the university (or college, or department) has on students using professional editors.
- Get on official proofreader lists (many universities have these).
- Create a flyer and post it on university noticeboards. You would have to seek permission to do this.
- Join a third-party provider that specialises in the proofreading of theses. There are a number of sites that perform this service, essentially acting as a link between students and proofreaders, but this guide is not the place to discuss their merits and demerits. If you simply google 'proofread thesis' or 'proofread dissertation', you will soon find a number of options, but do check that they are reputable and not an 'essay factory'.[1]

---

[1] An essay factory (or essay mill) is well described by Wikipedia as 'a business that allows customers to commission an original piece of writing on a particular topic so that they may commit academic fraud'. This practice, also known as contract cheating, is illegal in many countries. Regardless of the law, every university regards the use of an essay mill as extremely unethical and a student who does use one is at risk of severe punishment if caught.

2 | Working with students

Initial queries

Most queries on whether you can take on a thesis come in the form of an email. Consider the following two examples. If you had time to take on only one job, which one would you choose?

> *To: Editor*
> *From: AHara@kcl.ac.uk*
> *Date: 16 April*
>
> *Dear [your name]*
>
> *I wonder if you are available to help me proofread my thesis? Its title is 'Editing in a Digital World' and I estimate it will be about 25,000 words, including a dozen or so tables. I am writing the final chapter now, and plan to finish by 18 May. Deadline for submission is 30 June. I would be grateful if you could let me have an estimate of the cost.*
>
> *Thank you.*
>
> *Ada O'Hara*

Or ...

> *Hi, I want you to proofread my thesis for me. If I send on Monday, can you do by Thursday? Also, what is the costs?*
>
> *Bee, sent from my iPhone*

It goes without saying that the first email engenders much more confidence in the sender than the second one does. And if you have more confidence in the sender, you tend to have more confidence that the thesis itself will be more straightforward to work on. In effect, these emails represent the students taking the first step in the client/editor relationship, and the first email does it rather well, while the second does not. It is worth examining why.

2 | Working with students

	Email 1	Email 2
Medium	Ada's request has come in by email, using what looks like a valid university email address. This is a positive sign that a practical working relationship will be easy to establish.	Bee's request has come in via email from a mobile phone. Notwithstanding the growing use of mobile phones for business, this does mean that you will have to establish a more practical way of working, as it isn't feasible to work on a thesis, or work with an editor on the proofread of a thesis, on a phone.
Form of address	Ada's email is addressed to you personally. Even if Ada has written to other editors asking for quotes, this attention to detail is another positive sign.	Bee's 'Hi' lacks a personal touch and probably indicates this is a 'round robin' email. There is nothing wrong with seeking several quotes, of course, but a better impression would be given by at least addressing the query emails to the recipients by name.
Dates	Ada's email is dated 16 April, the thesis should be completed by 18 May, and final deadline is 30 June. All this leaves plenty of time to carry out a proofread and also reflects favourably on Ada's ability to plan ahead.	Although no dates are given, Bee wants to send the thesis next week and allows only four days, at best, to proofread it. This seems ambitious and sounds rushed, even if it turns out that the thesis is very short.
Information given	Ada gives the name of the thesis and roughly how long it is likely to be.	Bee gives no information at all about the thesis.
Tone and style	Ada's email is polite and well written. This bodes well for a future relationship and also for the level of proofreading required.	Bee's email seems rather abrupt and contains some grammatical errors. These may be warning flags – but see next page.

Warning flags

The two emails examined above are admittedly at either end of what you might call the assessment spectrum: you are unlikely to ever receive such a thoroughly well-written and useful enquiry as Ada's, but you would be equally unlikely to receive such a poorly written enquiry as Bee's. Be cautious about drawing too many conclusions from the apparent warning flags highlighted in the table. For example:

- Sending an email or text by phone rather than emailing with a computer is the preferred method of communication for many people nowadays.
- Do not assume that an abrupt style of email represents the character of the sender. English is not the first language of many students. They may not be used to phrasing requests of this sort in English; some students may not realise that some forms of address and some styles of writing are more polite than others.
- Do not assume that grammatical mistakes and spelling errors necessarily reflect the standard of writing in the thesis. We have all been guilty of dashing off an email or other form of message and, after pressing the send button, realising that it contains some errors.

That said, if a query email contains a number of warning signs, it would be as well to bear them in mind as you start to negotiate with your prospective client. They may affect the level of your fee, or even whether you decide to bid for the job at all.

Your response

At this stage the one thing a student always asks is, 'How much will it cost?', but this is the one question you cannot answer yet. Don't be tempted to give some answer such as, 'You say your thesis will be in the region of 25,000 words. My normal fee for a thesis of this length is £500.'

Your fee is based not on the number of words in the thesis (although obviously this is a factor), but on how long it takes you to carry out the proofread. The proofread of one 25,000-word thesis can, quite literally, take twice as long as the proofread of a different 25,000-word thesis.

Write back asking for any missing information, and explain that you cannot give a fee estimate until you have seen a sample of the thesis. Ask for 500 or 1,000 words; say that you will work through the sample, timing how long it takes, and then work out an estimate based on the result. Make the point that you will return the proofread sample along with your fee estimate, so that the student gets the chance to see what you can do.

Of course, if you send back the proofread sample and the student subsequently decides not to work with you, you'll have lost out on a bit of time. But working on a free sample and using it to estimate your fee is a good technique to employ (with any potential client where a fixed fee is not involved). In the same way that a well-written query email gives you confidence in whoever is enquiring, your proofread sample and willingness to send it will give the potential client confidence in you. Over time, you will find that working on these short samples is time well spent and good marketing practice.

Calculating fees

You can find out a lot about how to set fees in the CIEP guide *Pricing a Project*, but in fact pricing the proofread of a thesis is straightforward. There are three things to bear in mind:

- It is good practice to tell the student how you arrived at your estimate, not only in the interests of transparency, but also because they are more likely to accept an estimate if they understand how it was arrived at, rather than just being informed, 'The total fee is £416.' You can develop a standard paragraph along the lines of:

  It took me 25 minutes to work through the 750 words in the sample. This implies I can work through about 1,800 words in an hour. My hourly rate is £30.00, so assuming the thesis is 25,000 words in length, the total fee works out at £416 (£16.64 per thousand words).

  It's worth putting in the rate per thousand words, because that can be used as a yardstick if the thesis turns out to be a different length than originally anticipated.

- Make sure you make it clear that the sample should be representative. Ask for 'a representative sample' and, if you so wish, add a reminder in your fee email that 'it took 25 minutes to work through the representative sample'. It would be bad news to find that the sample was much easier to proofread than the thesis as a whole.
- Make sure you make it clear if formatting, styling references or proofreading appendices (if they are not included in the overall word count) are included in your estimate. Again, there is no harm in having a standard paragraph that can be added into your fee email, along the lines of:

   Please note that this estimate may vary if any work is required on formatting the thesis, checking the styling of references or working on any appendices (if they are not included in the overall word count).

There is more about formatting and references later in this guide, in the section on ethical considerations.

It is a common fear among proofreaders starting out on this kind of work that students are poor payers and might try to pay less than was agreed or get out of paying altogether. Anecdotal evidence over the years indicates that this is probably an unfounded suspicion: in fact, students usually pay more promptly than professional organisations, not being bound by the rigours of payment run timescales.

You can build in some safeguards against non-payment if you wish. The most common practice is to ask for 50% (or another percentage) of the payment upfront, with the remaining 50% due on completion. Another safeguard is to make sure you have the name and contact details of the student's supervisor before you start work. If the worst comes to the worst, you can always contact the supervisor to let them know that the student has not paid for professional services rendered: in fact, the mere threat of doing this may persuade the student client to pay up.

Requesting payment up front and asking for supervisor details will both then form a part of the agreement you make with the student, usually set out in an academic agreement, of which more in the following section.

Student agreement

Code of practice

During the early negotiations with the student, you will need to make it absolutely clear what it is you can and can't do within the ethical constraints of proofreading theses. One way of doing this is to draw up a standard code of practice that you can send with one of your early emails, asking the student to check what it says, and return a signed version or confirmation of acceptance.

The code of practice will be covered more thoroughly in the section on ethical considerations, but in summary, it would cover general issues (ranging from typographical errors to logic flow), indicating which can be covered by a proofread and which would remain the student's responsibility to deal with.

Academic agreement form

An academic agreement form is essentially a code of practice that incorporates the detail of the particular job you are currently negotiating.

So as well as the generic points mentioned above, it also includes the name and contact details of the student, the title of the thesis, the agreed fee, contact details for the supervisor and relevant dates.

Because the form includes details of the agreed fee, it is usually sent along with the fee email. A generic code of practice can be sent earlier – but then the practical details of the job at hand would have to be sorted out via an email instead.

There is no right or wrong way to deal with these matters. Some proofreaders prefer to send a generic code of practice and deal with contact details and fee amount by email; others prefer to wrap up everything in an academic agreement form.

Whichever method you decide to use, it is important to make sure that the student agrees to your fee amount and acknowledges the restrictions on your proofread. The academic agreement form will also be covered in more detail in the section on ethical considerations.

Timing

When you have carried out a proofread and sent the result back to the student, it may take them some time to deal with all your corrections, suggested changes and queries. This is obvious to you, but it might not be obvious to the student. It's therefore a good idea to point out to the student that they should build in some time before the thesis deadline to take account of this work.

You could say that you will return the thesis at least a week before the deadline. This means that the student has to get the thesis to you in good time to make this proofreading deadline.

Generally speaking, not everyone has excellent time and project management skills, and students sometimes struggle with these aspects of completing a thesis. As well as the relatively simple task of making sure there is enough time set aside to do whatever has to be done, you should also consider the following.

Workflow

There is likely to be a lot of back-and-forth communication between you and the student as you work through and come upon queries that the student has to answer before you can complete your proofread satisfactorily. Establish a way of working that ensures you don't get back the dreaded response, 'Thanks for these queries. I have changed the appropriate places in the thesis (copy attached) and made a few other changes as I was going through.'

This may make you smile, reading it in this guide, but it has happened many times, to both experienced and inexperienced proofreaders. Such a response leaves you floundering, not knowing which copy of the thesis to use, particularly if you have moved further on with the proofread while the student was making their unwelcome changes.

To prevent this sort of thing from happening, it is probably best to:

- explain very clearly to the student that this sort of situation must be avoided, and why
- refrain from sending back the actual thesis during the proofread – send a tabular list of queries instead, with an instruction to answer in the table, and not on any version of the thesis.

Version control

If for some reason it is necessary to send back the thesis, or parts of it, to the student as the proofread progresses, make sure that there is a clear form of version control in place. Perhaps add the date on the end of successive versions, or something like proof1, proof2, etc. This control can prove invaluable if, for example, a student is sending you their thesis on a chapter-by-chapter basis, possibly months in advance of the deadline.

Clearly, the student may want the proofread versions to hand as soon as you have completed them, not all at once days before the deadline. Equally clearly, you will want to keep track of what the latest versions are, so it is important for you to establish a form of version control (and share it with the student, so that they know what is going on).

By establishing these practical issues at the outset you will almost certainly save yourself time during the proofread: put simply, you will save yourself having to spend time trying to solve the problems that might otherwise be caused. Students are often not aware of how long tasks take, so it is good practice to estimate the actual time for the whole process (as against time actually spent on the proofread) generously, factoring in that things often go wrong.

Discussing this with the student as early as possible is important; if it's not discussed, the student may proceed with unrealistic expectations.

Working on the sample

There are a few points to remember when working through the sample:

- As noted earlier, in an ideal world you will be *proofreading* the sample – that is, checking for errors in spelling, punctuation, grammar and consistency, and pointing out awkward or ambiguous phrases. But the chances are that you will need to go further than this and carry out a proof-edit. You should have this in the back of your mind and allow for some flexibility; but if you find yourself drifting into a full copyedit or

even rewriting, then at the very least you should make a mental note that you will have to contact the student's supervisor. You may even decide to tell the student that the thesis is not ready for a proofread, and decline the job.
- Time yourself and use the result to calculate your fee. Don't be tempted to think, 'It took me half an hour to proofread these 1,000 words, but I expect I'll speed up when I have the whole thesis to work on. I'll quote on the basis of 25 minutes.' This is a bad idea. Your assumption might be wrong, in which case the thesis only has to reach 12,000 words for your quote to be underestimated by an hour. Or the full thesis might turn out to be slower work than you expected from the sample, perhaps because of consistency issues. You can live with this to some extent, but not if you have already shaved some time off what should have been your original estimate.
- If, based on the sample, you consider that there is going to be a lot of toing and froing with the student to sort out queries, consider adding on some time to the raw time estimate to take account of this extra work.
- If there are a lot of footnotes, ensure that they are included in the thesis word count.
- If there are a lot of references, make sure that your work on them is minimal at this stage: you will have to agree with the student what work (if any) you are to do on them, and charge this as a separate fee. The same thing goes for appendices, should there happen to be any in the sample.

Most of these points are straightforward. The one that is hardest to judge is how far to move away from proofreading towards editing. Just how much of an edit is a 'proof-edit', when working on a thesis?

The answer to this question lies in thinking about the ethical considerations.

3 | Ethical considerations

It has already been pointed out several times in this guide that a thesis should be the student's own work. To spell this out more clearly:

> *It must be remembered that a thesis – that is, some form of reasoned argument – is part of the examination for an MA, MSc or PhD degree, as is a dissertation for an undergraduate degree. Production of the thesis is part of the student's process of getting the degree. It is not your job as a proofreader to write, rewrite or, heaven forbid, 'ghost-write' a student's work. … If you are asked to do any of these things, you are ethically bound to decline such a job. Neither should you be making the student look 'better' than they are, academically, by rephrasing or making any substantial alterations to the text. Certainly any fact-checking or critique of data is not your job.*[2]

It would be delightful, and it would be straightforward, if a thesis presented to you needed only proofreading. In a sense it would also be straightforward if a thesis presented to you needed heavy editing: you shouldn't do it unless you have a frank exchange with the relevant supervisor and receive the go-ahead. The problem is that there is a large grey area in between, where it can be very difficult to decide whether it is all right to make or suggest a change, or whether it steps over the ethical red line.

To help to understand the problems more clearly, this section considers the following issues:

- plagiarism
- fact-checking and context
- artificial intelligence (AI)

[2] Taken from the CIEP course Proofreading Theses and Dissertations: **ciep.uk/training/choose-a-course/proofreading-theses-and-dissertations**.

- rewriting
- references
- formatting
- code of practice
- academic agreement.

Plagiarism

What is plagiarism exactly? The Oxford English Dictionary defines it as:

> [t]he action or practice of taking someone else's work, idea, etc, and passing it off as one's own; literary theft.

You can enjoy finding out more about plagiarism at the University of Sheffield's quiz (**librarydevelopment.group.shef.ac.uk/referencing.html**). Wikipedia also gives a lot of information about plagiarism, including details on the slightly counter-intuitive notion of self-plagiarism.

What might tip you off to the possibility that some part of a thesis is copied from somewhere else? Any one of the following might make you wonder:

- a change in writing style, especially if from ungrammatical to perfect English
- a change in spelling style, for example from UK to US spellings of some words

- use of technical terms or jargon that has not been previously used or defined
- a change in text font size or style
- hyperlinks or references in the text leading to what looks like the original material.

You might be wondering why plagiarism sits in a section on ethical 'grey areas'. It is clear that it shouldn't happen; the student should not plagiarise. But on the assumption that you do suspect plagiarism, the ethical problem that arises is: should you do anything about it?

Is it up to you, a proofreader, to put on a supervisor's or reviewer's hat and warn the student that part of what they have included in their thesis should probably be attributed to somebody else, and that not doing so is considered a form of cheating in academic circles? Or should you simply go about your business of checking spelling, grammar, punctuation … and steer clear of the problem, which is none of your making?

The problem is further compounded by the fact that the student may not know anything about plagiarism. They may think it perfectly acceptable to quote somebody without attributing it. Their academic institution should give guidance on plagiarism, but perhaps your client was not given such guidance, or failed to understand it, or simply didn't read it.

Perhaps the student always intended to attribute the piece of text that has attracted your attention, forgot to do so and will be grateful to you for pointing out the omission.

It is *not* the proofreader's job to look for or detect plagiarism. But if you do suspect it, should you do anything about it? A comparison can be drawn with auditors when they check client accounts. It is *not* the auditor's job to look for or detect fraud, but they would be failing in their duty if they uncovered fraud and said nothing about it. Likewise, you could be considered unprofessional if you spot potential plagiarism and say nothing about it.

3 | Ethical considerations

If you do come upon some text that you suspect might originate somewhere else, probably the best way forward is to raise a query. Highlight the worrisome piece of text and ask something like this:

> *I note that the second sentence of this paragraph appears to be written in a different style than the rest of the paragraph and the thesis as a whole. Should it be attributed to another writer? It is very important to acknowledge any text quoted from another writer or researcher.*

The query makes no judgement: you raise the query regardless of whether this is deliberate plagiarism, accidental plagiarism or not plagiarism at all. But pointing out the possible problem:

- helps the student by raising awareness about possibly doing something that could jeopardise their chances of obtaining their degree
- helps your professional reputation, should you fail to point out something that is obviously possible plagiarism and is subsequently picked up by a supervisor
- helps the academic institution itself, by indicating possible plagiarism being used in a thesis sponsored by that institution.

Once you have raised the query, you have done all you can do. You have no control over whether the student acts on your comment, or chooses to ignore it. Only in exceptional cases, in a thesis where there seems to be a lot of possible plagiarism and the student ignores your constant queries, would you go to the supervisor and tell them of your worry.

There is one other facet to possible plagiarism; that is, it might arise as a result of the student using artificial intelligence (AI), usually in the form of a chatbot, to write or enhance parts of their thesis. Using AI can cause a number of problems, which are dealt with separately on pages 26–28.

Fact-checking

You should not carry out any checks on statements or facts contained in a thesis. If you do, you are potentially impacting the *content* of the thesis, thereby crossing over the proofreading ethical red line.

Look at it another way. If you check a 'fact' in a thesis and discover it to be wrong, what would you do? It is clearly not appropriate or ethical to point the error out to the student, as doing so might help them attain their qualification. So why bother checking the 'fact' in the first place?

This does not mean that you are necessarily silent every time you spot something wrong or potentially wrong. There are occasions when it is appropriate to raise a query (as discussed below). But it does mean that you should not actively carry out any work to check something in a thesis.

Fact-querying

Your default position on querying a statement or a fact in a thesis is 'don't do it'. It's not much different from checking a fact, after all. But there are some occasions when it would seem perverse not to make a comment or query. For convenience, the rights and wrongs of fact-querying are divided here into three factors: common knowledge, context and impact, and typographical error.

Common knowledge

Consider the following sentence:

> *The largest planet in the solar system, Saturn, has a sidereal day of only 11 hours.*

That Jupiter and not Saturn is the largest planet in the solar system is common knowledge. Is it all right – is it ethically acceptable – to query this error? Yes. You do not have to 'fact-check' it, and it would be taking an extreme position to read such an obvious error and ignore it. *But you should not make any change.* You should never make any factual change in a thesis (unless it is a clear typographical error, as discussed later): in any case, here you do not know whether the student meant to say '... largest planet in the solar system, Jupiter ...' or '... the second-largest planet in the solar system, Saturn ...' Simply highlight the first part of the sentence and query, 'Is this right?'

It might now occur to you to wonder if the 11 hours is correct. Does 11 hours actually represent the sidereal day of Saturn? If so, it will have to be changed if the student changes Saturn to Jupiter. Or is it in fact the sidereal day of Jupiter? If so, it will need to be changed if the student decides to stick with Saturn. The planet name and the figure for the sidereal day need to match up.

If the sentence were contained in an academic book, or a journal paper, you would have no hesitation in flagging up the need to make sure the planet and the figure match. But you should not do this in a thesis. It is up to the student to make sure any figures quoted are accurate. Certainly you should not do any research to find out what the 11 hours actually refers to.

So the first part of this sentence contains an error that you, as a proofreader, can legitimately flag up with a query, because it is common knowledge. And the second part demonstrates facts that you should leave strictly alone.

Context and impact

Is it ethically acceptable to always comment on an error identified by 'common knowledge'? The answer to that is, as you might have come to expect by now, 'it depends'. Consider the following partial sentence:

> ... for example, Archimedes' discovery of gravity, or Faraday's experiments with electricity, or Einstein's thought experiments that led to his theory of relativity.

Here the relevant common knowledge is that Newton discovered gravity, not Archimedes. Your first instinct is probably to highlight the offending phrase and ask, 'Is this right?' But you must also consider the context in which the error has occurred.

Suppose the thesis is based on the idea that the types of discovery made at certain points in history are influenced by the political status of the state or country in which they are made. The thesis goes on to discuss the link between Archimedes' discovery of gravity and the Greek form of democracy that operated at that time. Now the 'common knowledge' error has assumed great importance: if you point this out to the student, they may be able to revamp their argument to take account of the error, or they may not.

But in either case, your comment has directly impacted the content of the thesis, and you have therefore crossed that ethical red line. You should remain silent.

Suppose instead the student is trying to set the scene for describing how scientific advancement frequently speeds up in the presence of genius, and in fact the thesis is going to concentrate on, let us say, Stephen Hawking and his theories about black holes and subsequent advances in cosmology. Archimedes never gets another mention. Now you might reasonably ask, 'Is this correct?', because making the necessary change has no effect on the thesis as a whole. Archimedes and his spurious connection to gravity was something of a throwaway line and could be deleted entirely without affecting the contentions in the thesis.

What this example goes to show is that the context of an error also has to be taken into account. If the thesis goes on to use the erroneous 'fact' to prove its contentions, then that thesis is based on faulty logic and will presumably struggle to make the grade. But that is not your concern: you are a proofreader, not a supervisor. To repeat: you should not do anything that impacts the content of a thesis, even if the error you have spotted is rooted in common knowledge.

Typographical error

Most typographical errors that lead to an error of fact are to do with numbers or dates. Consider the following three examples:

> *The so-called Norman Conquest was an invasion and occupation of England in 1966 by an army led by William the Conqueror.*
> *Everyone born after 2102 is entitled to make a claim, regardless of birthplace.*
> *Only 5 countries meet this criteria: France, Germany, Great Britain and Spain.*

The errors here are plain to see. The question is: is it ethical to point them out or make any change?

It is common knowledge that the Norman Conquest took place in 1066. This is a clear typographical error, and you should make a change.

Clearly 2102 is incorrect and it is inconceivable that making a correction will impact the content of the thesis. It is a typographical error very similar to that in the first example. But here you will have to make a query, as you do not know if the student meant 2012 or 2002.

Is the third a typographical error? It may be that the student intended to type 4 rather than 5, and if this were the only possibility you would feel justified in raising a query. But suppose there should in fact be five countries in the list, and the student has missed one out? The accidental omission of something from a list as straightforward as this one is unlikely to be critical to the content of the thesis. You should regard this as a normal proofreading error and flag up to the student that something has gone awry.

Fact-querying summary

It is worth taking a moment to summarise the proofreader's constraints when it comes to statements of fact that are incorrect:

- You should never carry out any *fact-checking*. It is up to the student to make sure the facts in a thesis are correct.

- If something that is common knowledge (ie it does not require fact-checking) is incorrect, you may *query* the statement to alert the student that something is wrong – but only if you judge that the context of the error is such that correcting it will not impact the content of or contentions in the thesis.
- Typographical errors that lead to a factual error usually relate to figures and generally it is ethically acceptable to query them (or in some cases, make a change).

Needless to say, the guidance in this list is just that – guidance. It is not a list of rules. It is guidance that attempts to reduce the size of that grey area around whether it is acceptable and ethical to change or query factual error, but that grey area will always be there. That is one of the beauties and one of the frustrations of proofreading theses: there is always something new waiting around the corner to confound us.

Artificial intelligence (AI)

It is clear that artificial intelligence (AI) is increasingly going to affect all our lives. This is certainly true for writers, editors and proofreaders, as chatbots get better and better at understanding the use of words, and people get better and better at using chatbots.

How is AI going to affect proofreading theses and dissertations?

Although it is too early to be sure, the perhaps surprising answer is – very little. On the assumption that you have been commissioned to proofread a thesis which has been partially constructed using AI (an assumption we will challenge later in this section), consider the following two problems.

1. Has the student used AI to generate material? If so, this new material might quote existing publications without acknowledgement (something chatbots have been known to do). In other words, are there instances of plagiarism in the thesis? Well, there might be, and it might be that the student has no idea that they are there, but as we have been at pains to point out earlier in this guide, it is the student's responsibility to acknowledge material used from elsewhere – that is, to avoid plagiarism.

It is not your responsibility. It would be sensible to make sure the student is aware of the possibility of plagiarism creeping in if a chatbot has been used – perhaps as part of the agreement explained later in this guide – but, apart from that, you can safely ignore what we might call the 'AI plagiarism effect' on a thesis.

2. Has the student used AI to generate material for their thesis which turns out to be incorrect? Well, possibly, but as we have also been at pains to point out in this guide, you have no responsibility for the content of a thesis. You should actively steer clear of making any comment on the contents. So, you can also safely ignore what we might call the 'AI accuracy effect' on a thesis.

So far, the fact that a student might use AI to help in the production of a thesis has had no discernible effect on the subsequent proofreading of that thesis. (Although it is worth pointing out that the same is not true of most other materials, where strict rules about the author being responsible for all content do not apply.) However, there is a third consideration: that is, has the student written some material and then asked a chatbot to check it through for grammar, spelling and punctuation and to 'improve the writing'? This amounts to asking a chatbot to act as a proofreader and/or copyeditor.

Using AI as proofreader

Suppose a student inputs whatever they have written into a chatbot and asks it to 'correct spelling, grammar and punctuation using Hart's Rules as guidance' – or a similar instruction. In other words, 'Chatbot, please proofread this.'

Is this acceptable practice under the relevant university's rules? Your first reaction might be, 'No, of course not.' But stop and think about it for a moment. Students are already able to use Word's Editor, macros within Word, PerfectIt and Grammarly, to name a few of the most visible available writing aids. Is using a chatbot really any different? It is beyond the remit of this guide to discuss this issue in detail, but a proofreader about to proofread a thesis should find out what position the relevant university takes on using AI in this fashion.

To put it another way, if the relevant university allows theses to be professionally proofread, does it really matter if you or a chatbot does the proofreading? And a student may just assume that the chatbot has done the job – quite possibly, for free – so why bother hiring a pair of human eyes? At the start of this section we said we would challenge the idea that you, as a human proofreader, might be commissioned to proofread a thesis which has been partially constructed using AI. In a future where 'proofreading by AI' is an accepted practice, it will probably be an unfortunate reality that the opportunities for human proofreaders to work on theses are likely to drop away as AI becomes better at proofreading and students become better at utilising AI.

The bottom line here is that you should ascertain whether the university allows theses to be proofread. The fact that a student might have used a chatbot to tidy up their text before submitting it to you (if you are lucky enough to be commissioned in this way) is irrelevant.

Using AI as copyeditor

Lastly, let's suppose a student has written something and asked a chatbot to 'make this read better', or some similar instruction. In other words, 'Chatbot, please copyedit this.'

As usual, the first thing to do is to ascertain if this has happened, and then to find out what position the university takes on copyediting. More and more universities are starting to issue guidance on the use of AI for the writing of theses. But if there is no strict guideline, you should contact the supervisor for their view. It may be that for a heavily scientific thesis full of equations and formulas, the supervisor takes the view that there isn't much text and its importance to the thesis is minimal, so go ahead and use a copyeditor (human or AI). On the other hand, using AI copyediting for a thesis dealing with language or the social sciences, where the formulation of arguments in text is important, might not be acceptable.

Rewriting

You should not carry out any rewriting in a thesis.

The closest you can get to it is if a thesis is written very poorly, so poorly that every sentence is a muddle and has to be unscrambled before it makes any sense. Such theses do crop up from time to time.

If you judge that only heavy editing can save the thesis, you may decide to contact the supervisor and explain the position. In the interests of courtesy and maintaining a

good working relationship, you would normally tell the student that you plan to do so, and why. You should not carry out heavy editing unless the supervisor is aware of what is happening. You should also make sure that the student knows that they are responsible for the content of the thesis and for checking that your changes have not accidentally changed the intended meaning.

If you judge that even heavy editing will not save the thesis, you should refuse the job and explain that the thesis is not yet in good enough condition for proofreading. On very rare occasions you might not become aware of the need for a rewrite until after you have gone through the process of working on a sample and making an arrangement to do the work. This might happen if the sample proves not to be representative of the thesis as a whole; that is why you should specify in your academic agreement that the sample must be representative, and you reserve your rights to increase your price or decline the job altogether if it turns out not to be.

References

There is nothing intrinsically wrong with helping a student to set out and format their references. You can carry out a check that there is a citation for every reference, and vice versa.

There are four things to watch out for:

- You should not help by looking up references, or checking that names, dates etc are correct in a reference. This is akin to fact-checking and crosses the ethical red line.
- As noted above, you can check there is a citation for every reference, and vice versa. But if you start this task and discover that there are a lot of mismatches, then you should call a halt. It is the student's responsibility to give a complete set of references, not yours. One or two citations without references, or vice versa, are mechanical errors and there is nothing wrong with pointing them out. But any more than that is a problem: by highlighting all the omissions you are helping the student to compile their reference list, and that also transgresses the red line.
- The student is responsible for checking that references and citations follow whatever style is preferred by their academic institution. You should ask if there is such a preferred style. If there is, you can proofread the references to make sure they follow that style, but it is not your job to carry out a wholesale reformat of them. (Although you may agree to do so if there are only a handful of references.)
- Working on references, especially their formatting, can be a laborious process. It is best to quote separately for carrying out this work. Very often, when you do that, students have a change of heart and decide to check the references themselves.

Formatting

There is nothing intrinsically wrong with helping a student with the formatting of their thesis. There are three points to watch out for:

- There is no ethical problem in, for instance, checking the numbering system, ensuring the capitalisation of headings is consistent and

even drawing up an automatic contents page. But it is the student's responsibility to create the numbering system and the wording for the headings: you should not be doing that.
- The student is responsible for providing you with a formatting guide from their academic institution, if there is one. Ask if there is such a guide.
- As for references, working on formatting can be a laborious process. It is best to quote separately for carrying out this work. Again, as for references, very often when you do that, students have a change of heart and decide to format the thesis themselves.

Code of practice

As noted near the start of this guide, it is advisable to have to hand a code of practice that sets out in general terms what you can do as a proofreader, and what you cannot. The example on the next page is taken from the CIEP online course **Proofreading Theses and Dissertations**. As noted earlier in this guide, the advantage of this type of code of practice is that it is generic and can be sent out to any student client at any stage during negotiations. It can be sent out before an agreement on fee has been reached – before an agreement to carry out the work at all has been reached. In effect, it points out the ethical red lines to the student and is an invaluable step in their introduction to the world of the professional proofreader.

[your logo]	**Code of Practice: Editing Masters and PhD theses**	
The following restrictions apply to proofreading/editing work undertaken on manuscripts that are to be submitted for examination.		

Proofreading/editing activities		Checked and corrected **by the editor**	May be highlighted by the editor **for correction by the student***
Level 1: Proofreading	Typographical errors	✓	
	Spelling	✓	
Level 2: Minor editing	Grammar	✓	
	Inconsistencies in language	✓	
	Clarity		✓
Level 3: Stylistic/ structural editing (see panel below)	Repetitions		✓
	Logic flow		✓

* Specific queries may be raised by the editor for the student to address. However, no actual rewriting can be done by the editor on examined texts.

I understand and agree to the limits described above for editorial work on manuscripts that are to be submitted for examination, and that the editor is not responsible for the outcome of the exam.

This work is undertaken with the knowledge and consent of my supervisor and/or thesis committee.

Student's signature: Date:

Structural editing

Repetitions

If a student has used the same sentence or paragraph more than once, word for word, it is reasonable to point this out. This is a weakness or error in writing, not in the underlying ideas put forward in the thesis. The proofreader can point out any such repetitions for the student to think about and change if they think it necessary.

Logic flow

Note that a proofreader will not normally make any structural suggestions relating to the text. But on the rare occasions when it has been agreed with the supervisor that the thesis requires more heavy editing (which occasionally happens, as noted in the section on rewriting) the proofreader may sometimes make suggestions to improve the way in which the text is laid out or ordered.

For example, the student may have written 'There are a number of interesting possibilities relating to spaceflight to Jupiter and Saturn', and then had a short section on Saturn followed by another on Jupiter – that is, writing out the possibilities in the opposite order to the way they are mentioned in the text.

The proofreader should not make a change here, as that would amount to rewriting, but could suggest to the student that they could reverse the order either of the text mentions or of the short following sections.

It is important to note that this type of 'logic flow' refers to the text and its clarity, not to the underlying thesis that the student is putting forward for their qualification.

Academic agreement

An academic agreement is merely a combination of a code of practice and the details of the job. It does not add anything further to the ethical issues surrounding proofreading theses, but this guide would be incomplete without any mention of what it is and what it contains.

In summary, an academic agreement could be structured as follows:

- Details on the quoted fee, along the lines of:
  The fee for onscreen proofreading/editing the thesis/dissertation, based on the sample you have sent me, is £x per 1,000 words. For the xxx words proposed, this equates to £xxx. This is subject to the following conditions:
  1. *The sample is representative of the whole. I reserve the right to change the price quote if the full text varies significantly from the sample.*
  2. *I do not advise on content, but restrict myself to making the meaning clear.*
  3. *I will need your confirmation that you have received authorisation from your supervisor to get such help as I provide. Ideally, your dissertation/thesis should contain an acknowledgement stating that it has been professionally edited (and by whom), especially if it is to be published.*[3]
- Details of the work to be carried out, including any separate agreements for working on references or formatting.
- Code of practice.
- Indicate what use has been made of artificial intelligence (eg a chatbot) in the writing of the manuscript; say 'None' if AI has not been used. Ask for confirmation that any use of AI conforms with university guidelines, or to state 'None' if no such guidelines exist.

---

[3] Taken from the CIEP course **Proofreading Theses and Dissertations**.

- Practical details:
  - » Name
  - » Address
  - » Telephone number
  - » Title of dissertation/thesis
  - » Approximate length
  - » Examining body
  - » Supervisor name
  - » Supervisor contact details
  - » Estimated date(s) for sending material for proofing
  - » Estimated date(s) required for return of material
  - » Final deadline.

4 | Summary

This guide has covered a lot of ground, but here is a summary of the main points.

- In an ideal world, you would proofread a thesis. In the real world, the work often leans towards editing, and very often you end up 'proof-editing'.
- Never undertake a heavy edit without supervisor consent.
- Working with students often entails teaching them how to work with a professional proofreader. Be careful how you deal with queries and possible warning flags in student communications.
- Don't be tempted to give a fee price too early, and don't be tempted to underestimate your fee.
- The thesis must be the student's own work. This gives rise to ethical dilemmas peculiar to the proofreading of theses:
  » Does anything look like possible plagiarism?
  » Never fact-check.
  » Query statements of fact only if they are common knowledge and do not fundamentally impact the thesis content.
  » Never rewrite.
  » It is ethically acceptable to work on references or on the formatting of a thesis – although even here there are constraints – but be clear about whether such work is included in your fee estimate.
- Create a code of practice (or academic agreement) to be used as part of your negotiating tactics.

5 | The next step

This guide has introduced some of the basic principles of proofreading theses and dissertations. In many respects, the work required is the same as for any other proofread – you check for errors in spelling, punctuation, grammar and consistency – but it is complicated by the fact that the thesis or dissertation must be the student's own work.

But this guide in itself can't equip you fully to undertake professional work. We have written an online course that covers the content of this guide in more depth and introduces more considerations. It takes you through the steps needed to successfully gain and work through a job of proofreading a thesis or dissertation.

You will find full details of the course on our website:

ciep.uk/training/choose-a-course/proofreading-theses-and-dissertations

There are ten exercises throughout the course, giving you plenty of practice at honing your skills. Each section includes study notes and a commentary on the exercises, with examples and model answers where appropriate.

By the end of the course you will:
- understand the ethical issues that come with working on theses or dissertations
- be able to communicate clearly with students and their supervisors about the work
- be able to negotiate an appropriate fee for the work

- have learned new skills that will help you to decide whether to take on a proofreading job
- understand the different formats in which a thesis or dissertation may be presented
- be able to provide feedback to your student clients and/or their supervisors.

About the author

Stephen Cashmore is a proofreader, editor and published writer based in Ayr, Scotland. He is an Advanced Professional Member of the CIEP, and for five years was training director of the SfEP, the CIEP's predecessor, during which time he developed and contributed to many of our online training courses (including Proofreading Theses and Dissertations).

Originally trained as a mathematician, he has had a variety of careers, including teacher and auditor, but he took early retirement in 2012 to train up as a proofreader, and wishes he had done so earlier. You can find out more about him at his websites:

cashmoreeditorial.com
and **stephencashmore.com**

Acknowledgements

With thanks to the following people who reviewed the draft of this guide and provided helpful advice and comments.

Dr Stephen Pigney

Ivan Butler MBA, CMIIA, **coachhousebusinessservices.co.uk**

Dr Peter Norrington, **linkedin.com/in/peternorrington**

Cathy Tingle, CIEP information team

www.ingramcontent.com/pod-product-compliance
Lightning Source LLC
Chambersburg PA
CBHW052107110526
44591CB00013B/2394